Vegetables
for Pots and Patios

FREIDRICH-W. FRENZ AND
THOMAS JAKSCH

Series Editor:
LESLEY YOUNG

MEREHURST

Introduction

Contents

Decorative and useful plants

The delicate green of lettuces growing beside bright red tomatoes and the red stalks of spinach beet pushing upward among tall maize cobs just go to show that, when cleverly arranged, many vegetables are just as decorative as ornamental plants. They can also be grown just as easily in tubs and containers. When they are artistically combined with scented herbs and luxuriantly blooming summer annuals, a colourful garden can be created in even the smallest space, which will not only provide visual pleasure but will also please your taste buds. In this book, authors Friedrich-W. Frenz and Thomas Jaksch provide a comprehensive guide to growing vegetables in containers. They recommend particularly suitable and attractive species and give easy-to-follow, tried and tested instructions on growing, care and harvesting. Imaginatively arranged planting examples will provide you with plenty of ideas for designing with vegetables, flowers and herbs. Just how attractive such plantings can be is shown in the excellent photographs taken specially for this volume.

Vegetables, herbs and summer flowers work well together.

A brilliant yellow gourd flower.

The flower of the runner bean.

The authors
Dr Friedrich-W. Frenz is
Professor of Garden Design at
the Fachhochschule
Weihenstephan in Freising and
also Head of the Institute for
Vegetable Cultivation. Thomas
Jaksch has studied garden
design and is the Managing
Director of the institute. Both
are enthusiastic growers of
vegetables in containers.

The photographers
Jürgen Stork, a well-known
nature and plant photographer,
took most of the photographs
for this guide. Other
photographs are by various
plant photographers (see
p. 61).

The illustrator
György Jankovics is a
professional graphic artist. He
studied at the academies of art
of Budapest and Hamburg and
is regularly commissioned to
produce animal and plant
subjects for a number of well-
known publishers. He has also
illustrated a number of titles in
the "Success with ..." series.

NB: Please read the Authors'
Notes on page 61 so that your
enjoyment of growing
vegetables in containers may
not be impaired.

Position and choice

It does not matter if you grow bushy
cherry tomato plants or vigorously
climbing runner beans – provided the right
position is chosen many attractive and
tasty vegetables will flourish in
containers. Both familiar old favourites
and exotic varieties are eminently suitable
for growing on balconies and patios.

*Left: Garden ornaments amid a luxuriant display of
plants.*
*Top: Gourd plants produce decorative fruit but
require a lot of space.*

Position and choice

Vegetable cultivation through the ages

Vegetables play a most important part in our daily menu and have always formed a major component of the human diet. Some of the earliest evidence of the importance of vegetables can be derived from the existence of paintings of vegetables found in Egyptian tombs.

From later periods of history, we have, for example, written instructions by Charlemagne (AD 742-814), establishing which species of vegetables were to be grown on his country estates. In the later Middle Ages, it was in monastery gardens, in particular, that the cultivation of vegetables, fruit and herbs was taken very seriously.

The Romans, and later the Moors, brought many species of vegetable, such as spinach and lettuce, from the Mediterranean area to northern and central Europe. Numerous useful plants that we now take for granted as part of our daily diet originally came from South or Central America, being first imported after the discovery of the Americas. This list includes tomatoes, beans and maize. Nowadays, as people travel extensively in many different parts of the world, we are constantly "discovering" new, hitherto unknown vegetables that we can use in recipes at home. It is particularly thrilling to grow such exotic plants oneself and to use them in the kitchen to create wonderful new dishes.

Vegetables in containers

Of course, vegetables are mainly grown in open soil. However, many tasty species and varieties can also be grown in containers without any great problems, and some have been specially raised for growing on balconies. If they are given a sunny, sheltered position, watered regularly and supplied with the required nutrients, vegetables will provide a rich harvest even on a patio or balcony.

You will, of course, never become self-sufficient as a vegetable gardener with only a balcony or patio. Nevertheless, your daily menu can be effectively enriched with the fruits of your potted plant garden. The flavour of a tomato that has ripened on the plant in the sun just cannot be compared with the taste of commercially produced tomatoes that are harvested when they are half-ripe and then ripened in storage.

Taste and colour

In practice, it is rarely the practical side of vegetable growing that is the most important factor for the balcony and patio gardener. Usually, it is simply the joy of gardening – the pleasure of seeing seeds germinate and watching them develop into fine flowering, fruit-producing plants. Last but not least, it is the ornamental value of many vegetable plants – their interesting growth and the colourful and strange shapes of the fruits – that compels balcony and patio gardeners to grow these useful plants. Even the flowers of many species of vegetable, such as those of the artichoke, the courgette or mange-tout, can easily be compared in beauty with those of other flowering plants.

If even this is not colourful enough for you, you can combine your vegetables with cheerful summer flowers and scented herbs. If they are well chosen, the latter will also supply the right flavours to add to the vegetables when you put them on the menu. Browse through the numerous planting examples in this book and try out different variations to suit yourself. If you find that you really enjoy growing vegetables in pots, you can create different arrangements each year with new species and different companion plants. Such a planting will never look boring.

A summery balcony box with vegetables and flowers. The dominant position in the background is taken up by the sweetcorn plant with its vigorous upward growth. In the centre are various leafy lettuce varieties, and trailing over the front are bush tomatoes and lobelia.

Leaf lettuces require a lot of light but are sensitive to high temperatures.

Lots of light and warmth

Plants require a position where they can feel at home just as they would in their natural environment. In contrast to flowers and herbs, there are hardly any species among the vegetables that either prefer or will even tolerate shade. The brighter and sunnier the position, the more luxuriant the growth of the plants and the earlier and more abundant the harvest. In permanent shade, for example, on a north-facing balcony, the harvest will inevitably be sparse. The most undemanding vegetables with respect to the amount of light they require are lettuce, spinach and spinach beet but even they need at least a semi-shady position. Most herbs are hungry for sun and prefer a light, warm position. This is particularly true for the Mediterranean herbs like basil, marjoram, rosemary, sage and thyme. Borage, dill, parsley, chives and lemon balm, on the other hand, will also thrive in semi-shady positions. They will, therefore, cope well when planted in the shade of larger plants.

Among the summer flowers for

balconies and patios, you will find species and varieties that are suitable for all types of position. Before you buy any plants, enquire about their requirements for light and warmth. A selection of sun-loving balcony flowers can be found on page 25.

The right position

The best positions for growing vegetables are those facing south west and south east. Completely south-facing balconies offer optimal conditions of light but during high summer they are usually too hot. While particularly warmth-loving species like tomatoes, peppers and aubergines will show their gratitude with a rich harvest of fruit, great heat will bother lettuce plants considerably during the hottest summer months. The lettuce will react by "bolting" and producing shoots and will burn inwardly. No matter what you grow, regular watering will be a most important factor in any south-facing position.

Exposure to wind

As well as taking note of plants' varying requirements with respect to light and temperature, you must remember that wind and draughts also play an important role if plants are to thrive. In general, vegetable plants prefer a wind-sheltered spot. Species with large or soft leaves, like cucumbers, melons and beans, are particularly sensitive to wind. They will react to any strong breeze or draught by wilting, especially if they are also in a dry medium.

If the position and the amount of light are adequate, you should stand your plant containers in the shelter of a wall or railing. Wherever this is not possible, reed mats or curtains made of firm fabric will provide protection from wind. Espaliers of climbing plants will also keep off the wind. In a sheltered position, the soil will not dry out so quickly; this will also reduce the need for watering.

On the other hand, a closed-in, completely windless site may become a breeding ground for fungal diseases. A light movement of air will allow damp leaves to dry off faster and will encourage healthy plants.

A medium strong current of air will also improve pollination and thereby ensure a more abundant harvest for many fruiting vegetables like tomatoes, peppers and sweetcorn.

Rain and wet leaves

Sites that face west are most exposed to wind and rain in stormy weather or during thunderstorms. The same goes for balcony boxes hanging on the outside of railings or for open rooftop gardens. For many vegetables, protracted periods of wet leaves due to rain are the main cause of diseases in leaves or fruit. Lettuces and cucumbers are more likely to be infested with downy mildew, and tomatoes by foot and root rot. In positions that are much exposed to rain it would be wiser to avoid growing vegetable species that are particularly sensitive to wet conditions. You will find advice and suggestions on this among the plant descriptions on pages 14-23.

Balconies close to heavy traffic

Should your balcony be situated close to a very busy road, it would be advisable to give up the idea of planting vegetables altogether and restrict yourself to flowers. This will prevent the possibility of you ingesting any toxic substances that might accumulate in the tissues of your home-grown vegetables.

Position and choice

Attractive plant containers can be made from a variety of materials.

Tomatoes in a terracotta pot.

Plant containers for a mobile garden

Once you have decided that your balcony or patio is suitable for the growing of vegetables, you will need to start looking for the right containers. The range of materials, shapes and sizes on offer is truly immense.

Clay is the classic material for plant containers. Ceramic containers come in the most varied shapes and sizes, unglazed or glazed. Pottery bowls, terracotta urns or simple clay pots are often real ornaments in themselves, even without any plants in them. Pocket amphoras made of clay (used for strawberry plants) are particularly decorative and can be planted with lettuce and herbs (see p. 45).

Wood has long been used for balcony tubs, large plant containers and planting boxes. Wood insulates well but is also sensitive to moisture. It will decay at varying rates depending on the type of wood. With a minimum of do-it-yourself skills, however, you can even build such rustic containers yourself. In order to protect the wood against rotting, it should be treated beforehand with environmentally friendly, biological agents.

Containers made of basketwork that can be placed on the ground or hung on a wall will harmonize well with vegetables. If they are not already lined with polythene, you can obtain thin polythene inserts to protect the basketwork from damp and mould.

Our tip: If you intend standing basket containers on the ground, you should place small spacers underneath to prevent them from decaying from below.

Reconstituted concrete containers are particularly durable.

Plastic containers are available in green, brown, white, grey and black. Plastic is a very lightweight material, very durable and very cheap. Remember, however, that dark-coloured plastic containers, in particular, tend to heat up considerably in the sun. Recently, attractive, light, "terracotta" plastic containers have appeared on the market, that are hardly distinguishable from genuine clay containers.

Containers made of cellulose fibres are environmentally friendly. They come in the most varied shapes and sizes. The manufacturers usually guarantee that they will last for about two years.

Pot holders: You can always make unattractive containers disappear inside beautiful pot holders. These usually do not have a drainage hole, however, so do make sure, therefore, that excess water from watering or rainfall is regularly emptied out of them.

The right size of container

It is better to choose a pot that is a little too large rather than one that is too small, as vegetable plants need plenty of space for their roots in order to produce a good harvest. This will also provide more stability and prevent the pot from tipping over. Larger containers also hold a larger supply of water and nutrients.

In the case of balcony boxes, you should ensure that they are not too heavy. Boxes with a length of 80 cm (32 in) should be about right. Individual containers with a capacity of 5-15 litres (9-26 pints) will be large enough for big plants like tomatoes, cucumbers or maize. If you want to move heavy containers around occasionally, you should be able to buy a rolling palette that will enable you to move heavy objects around very easily and without straining your back.

Drainage

It is particularly important for all plant containers to have drainage holes so that excess water can run away and no waterlogging can occur (see pp. 48-9). If necessary, cover the drainage holes with pot shards or large pieces of stone so they will not become clogged up with compost and excess water can run away unhindered. Many plant containers also come equipped with plant saucers that sit underneath them to prevent the formation of puddles of water around the pots.

Saving space when installing containers

If you wish to stand several large containers together without using up too much space, metal plant steps are very useful. They can be bought in many sizes in the garden trade. The step-like arrangement has the added advantage that all the plants will receive enough light.

Choosing your plants

If you are growing vegetables on a balcony or patio you will probably be very keen to have interesting shapes of growth, attractive flowers and tasty, unusual fruits. The following pages describe a range of decorative species of vegetables that are particularly suitable for cultivation in large containers. With most of the plants introduced here, harvesting is possible over a longish period of time, so you will be able to enjoy your patio garden all summer long.

In addition to information about the origins and botany of these plants, the descriptions given here also provide details of requirements of position and care, tips for successful cultivation and the correct methods of harvesting and use. Several useful culinary herbs are also covered as well as some colourful summer flowers that make ideal companion plants for vegetables. You will find other popular species in the planting and harvesting tables on pages 26-7, which will enable you to put together a varied planting plan of your own choosing.

Many attractive and tasty vegetables can be grown on balconies and patios.

Tomato

Lycopersicon lycopersicum

Family: Nightshade (*Solanaceae*).
Origin: South America, Andes regions.
Botany: A fruit-forming vegetable that is popular but very sensitive to frost. Profusely branching with masses of fruit. A distinction is made between tall-growing stick tomatoes and low-growing bush tomatoes. From the last month of spring onwards small yellow flowers appear in open clusters that develop into small green fruits within about two months and then turn yellow, orange or red. There is a large range of tomato plants on offer in garden centres in varying shades of colour, shapes and sizes (see p. 57).
Position: Full sunlight, warm and sheltered from wind. A dry position will prevent the formation of fungal diseases.
Propagating/planting: Sow seeds from the middle of the first month of spring at a temperature of at least 20°C (68°F). Sow very thinly so that strong seedlings will form. As soon as the first seed leaves are horizontal, prick out the small plants and plant them to just below their seed leaves in pots with a diameter of 10 cm (4 in).
Plants with damaged seed leaves should be discarded. Stand the seedlings in as bright a position as possible and make sure they are kept warm enough (about 18°C/64°F).
Later on the young plants should be placed in containers with a capacity of 5-10 litres (9-18 pints), planted no deeper than they were in the seedling pots to avoid decay of the stalks. From the middle of the third month of spring onwards, once no more frost is expected, stand the plants outside.
Our tip: If buying young tomato plants, make sure that the pots have a diameter of at least 8-10 cm (3½-4 in). In addition, the plants should have a strong stalk, low growth and display some early

Beef tomato "Rodeo"

flowerbuds. Further signs of health are green seed leaves and healthy roots.
Care: Tie tall-growing varieties to a stick or climbing frame (see p. 47). The best way of growing these plants is to encourage one shoot. The lateral shoots that appear in the leaf axils should then be pinched out regularly. Once five or six clusters of flowerbuds have appeared, take the top off the main shoot. There will not be enough time to allow further clusters of flowers to mature properly so they would only use up precious nutrients. Low-growing bush tomatoes should

Delicate tomato flowers.

not be tied up, trained or pinched out. A short stick will, however, provide stability if the clusters of fruit are very heavy.

Older, sick or yellow leaves should be removed regularly. Water plants often. If watering is done at irregular intervals, the tomato fruit will tend to split. Fertilize regularly. For a good harvest, occasionally shake the tomatoes so that pollen can fall on to the stigmas.

Plant protection: Foot and root rot is encouraged by wet foliage so keep the leaves as dry as possible.

Varieties: The following varieties are particularly suitable for growing in large containers.

● Tall-growing standard varieties: "Harzfeuer", "Tigarella" (red/yellow), "Goldene Konigin" (yellow), "Hellfrucht".

● Bush tomatoes: "Balkonstar", "Patio".

● Beef tomatoes: "Master", "Pyros" (both tall-growing).

● Cherry tomatoes: "Red Robin" (orange), "Gartenperle", "Minibel",

"Phyra", "Tumbler" as well as tall-growing varieties "Bistro", "Mirabel" (yellow) and "Sweet 100".

● Pear tomatoes: "Yellow Pear-shaped" (yellow, tall-growing).

● Egg-shaped tomatoes: "Roma" and "San Marzano" (tall-growing).

For hanging containers, choose the bush tomato: "Balkonstar" and cherry tomatoes "Red Robin", "Gartenperle", "Minibel", "Phyra" and "Tumbler".

Harvest: Harvest tomatoes when they are fully ripe and for immediate consumption. They should be juicy and firm to cut, have a high content of sugar, fruit acid, vitamin C, carotine and minerals and will, therefore, be particularly full of flavour. Never store tomatoes in the fridge – the best temperatures are 12-15ºC (54-59ºF).

Use: Tomatoes are particularly versatile. They can be used for salads, soups and sauces as well as for grilling.

Cherry tomatoes are particularly suitable for

Yellow plum tomatoes.

decorating salads and cold platters.

NB: While tomatoes are still green, they contain a toxic substance called solanin which gradually breaks down as the fruit ripens. Consume only fully ripe tomatoes.

Cherry tomatoes.

The white fruit of aubergine.

A purple pepper.

Aubergine, eggplant
Solanum melongena

Family: Nightshade
(*Solanaceae*).
Origin: India.
Botany: This plant is
very sensitive to frost. It
produces dark purple
fruit.
Position: Sunny, warm,
sheltered from rain and
wind.
Propagating/planting:
Early propagation from
the middle of the first
month of spring at 22-
24ºC (72-75ºF). Stand
the seedlings outside in
3-5 litre (5-9 pint)
containers from the end
of spring.
Care: Support will be
necessary if growth is
vigorous. Keep the
compost moist and
fertilize every two to
three weeks.
Varieties: "Black King",
"Baren" (longish-oval,
virus-resistant), "Galine"
(round-oval), "Adona"
(pear-shaped).
Harvest: Cut off the fruit
with scissors.
Use: Steamed, fried,
baked or grilled.
NB: Do not eat the fruit
raw as it contains the
toxin solanin.

Pepper
Capsicum annuum

Family: Nightshade
(*Solanaceae*).
Origin: Mexico, Peru.
Botany: Bushy, fruiting
vegetable. Sensitive to
cold. Two basic types:
vegetable peppers (mild)
and spicy paprika (hot).
Position: Sunny, warm,
out of wind and rain.
Propagating/planting:
From the beginning of
spring at 22ºC (72ºF).
From the middle of the
last month of spring plant
the seedlings in 3-5 litre
(5-9 pint) pots outside.
Care: Taller-growing
varieties should be
trained upwards. Excess
shoots should be
removed. Low-growing
varieties should be
allowed to grow bushy.
Remove the first flowers.
Keep the compost
moist. Fertilize every
three weeks.
Varieties: "Triton",
"Festival", "Sweet
Banana", "Pusztagold";
paprika: "Cayenne"
Harvest: When green or
fully ripe if coloured.
Use: Peppers can be
used raw or baked;
paprika as hot flavouring.

Cape gooseberry
Physalis peruviana

Family: Nightshade (*Solanaceae*).
Origin: Peru.
Botany: Sensitive to frost. It bears cherry-sized, orange-yellow fruit in papery cases.
Position: Full sunlight; dry, warm and sheltered from wind.
Propagating/planting: Sow from the middle of the first month of spring. Also propagated from cuttings. Only place young plants outside from the middle of the last month of spring.
Care: Cut back plants early and train up several vigorous shoots. Only cut out a few shoots. Water plentifully until the end of summer and fertilize every two weeks. Overwintering in a bright, cool position is possible (8-10°C/46-50°F). Cut back in the last month of winter.
Plant protection: If infestation with white fly occurs, employ *Encarsia* wasps (see pp. 54-5).
Harvest: Pick only orange-yellow fruit.
Use: Cape gooseberries taste bitter-sweet. They contain plenty of vitamin C and provitamin A, as well as iron and calcium. They can be made into jam and preserves or eaten raw.

Pepino or pear melon
Solanum muricatum

Family: Nightshade (*Solanaceae*).
Origin: Colombia.
Botany: A fruiting vegetable that is extremely sensitive to frost. It produces egg-shaped, yellow fruit with violet stripes.
Position: Sunny but not too warm; 15-20°C (59-68°F) is ideal.
Propagation/planting: Propagate from cuttings which root very easily. From the first month of spring onward, plant selected shoots, and set them in individual 10 cm (4 in) pots after three weeks. From the middle of the last month of

A pepino melon.

The Cape gooseberry has exotic flowers and delicious fruit.

spring, put three or four plants outside in a 5-litre (9 pint) container or in a hanging container with a diameter of 25 cm (10 in).
NB: When hanging up containers or balcony boxes, remember to estimate the weight of the fully grown plants plus damp compost.
Care: For hanging plants and balcony boxes, cultivate the plants to be bushy. To do this, pinch out the shoot tips in order to encourage early branching out. Otherwise train pepino plants upwards using two or more shoots. Pinch out the lateral shoots and train up the main shoots.
Overwintering is possible in a bright, cool but frost-free position. Cut back in the last month of winter.
Variety: "Pepino Gold".
Harvest: Not until the fruit begins to turn yellow (from the middle of the last month of summer).
Use: Raw like melons, bitter-sweet when steamed, as jam or jelly.

Position and choice

Lettuce
Lactuca sativa

Family: *Compositae.*
Origin: Mediterranean area, Egypt.
Botany: A distinction is made between lettuce for cutting, lettuce heads, iceberg lettuce, lettuce for picking and various other forms.
● Picking and cutting lettuces are good for cultivation in balcony boxes and pots. They form loose leaf rosettes and continue to grow if they are not completely harvested.
● Lettuce heads form larger, firmish heads. Miniature varieties are suitable for boxes and pots.
● Iceberg lettuce has large, firm heads with crisp leaves and leaf ribs.
● Batavia lettuce has softer leaves and forms loose, slightly fringed heads.
● Radicchio is a variety of lettuce from Italy with green and white or red and white heads. It does, however, require a longer cultivation period than picking lettuce and should not be sown out before the beginning of summer.

Position: Sunny and sheltered in spring and autumn. Also semi-shady in the summer. Avoid extreme heat above 30ºC (86ºF).
Growing: Early sowing is possible from the last month of winter onwards. Sow until the last month of summer. Picking lettuce should be sown thinly and the seedlings pricked out and replanted in pots with a diameter of 4 cm (under 2 in) or in small seed trays after about eight days. Depending on the time of year, the young plants should be ready to plant after three to five weeks and can be put out from the second month of spring onward. Cutting lettuce can be sown in the container in which it will grow. In balcony boxes, two rows per box can be sown quite easily. In a pot, sprinkle the seed about. Cover the seed with a very thin layer of compost and keep it evenly moist until germination occurs. Provided the weather is clement, lettuce for cutting can be placed in a sheltered position outside from the second month of spring onward.

Lettuce for picking can be harvested over a longer period of time.

Our tip: On very hot summer days, stand sown seed in a cool place for a day or two (cellar or fridge).
Planting: Look for short, vigorous growth when planting young plants. Always plant seedlings with the entire ball of compost around the roots. Only sink half the ball of roots into the compost so that the plant cannot decay from below.
A pot for a single lettuce head should have a diameter of 13 cm (5 in) or more. You may fit up to eight plants in a balcony box with a length of 80 cm (32 in), depending on the type of lettuce.
Care: If there is a risk of frost, protect the plants

Iceberg lettuce.

at night with a layer of fabric, polythene sheeting or newspapers. Water lettuce regularly but fertilize sparingly.

Plant protection: To prevent fungal disease, water lettuce in the mornings so that the leaves can dry off quickly.

Varieties: Some varieties are more apt to bolt (begin shooting) than others. Read the information given on the seed packet. Ask a nursery gardener for lettuce varieties with higher resistance to downy mildew. Red varieties are generally less infested by aphids than light green ones.

● Picking lettuce: "Till" (light green, pointed leaves), "Lollo bionda" (yellow-green, curly leaves), "Lollo rossa" (red, crinkly leaves); "Raisa" (red curly lettuce); "Krizet" (green, curly lettuce); "Frisby" (green, fine curly lettuce), "Carnival" (red-green oak leaf lettuce), "Brunia" (red oak leaf lettuce), "Salad Bowl" (yellow-green oak leaf lettuce with a thin leaf), "Red Salad Bowl" (red oak leaf lettuce with a thin leaf).

Radicchio, a colourful red lettuce from Italy.

● Cutting lettuces: "Gelber Runder", "Krauser Gelber". (All of the picking lettuces named above are also suitable as cutting lettuce.)

"Lollo rossa".

● Head or cabbage lettuces: "Barbarossa" (red), "Tom Thumb" (light green, mini head lettuce), "Sucrine" (light green, mini head lettuce).

● Batavia lettuce: "Grazer Krauthäuptl" (green-red), "Sioux" (red-brown), "Grands Rapids Salli" (yellow-green).

Harvest: From the beginning of the last month of spring to the first frosts.

● In the case of picking lettuce, the outer leaves can be regularly removed while new leaves are growing inside. The heart should always be left to continue growing.

● Cutting lettuces should be cut off with a sharp knife three to five weeks after sowing. If you allow 2-3 cm (¾-1¼ in) to remain, several harvests will be possible.

Use: Lettuce contains many vitamins, minerals and fibre. Intensely red varieties usually contain fewer nitrates than green varieties.

Cucumber
Cucumis sativus

Family: *Cucurbitaceae.*
Origin: India.
Botany: A fruiting vegetable that requires plenty of warmth. It produces yellow male and female flowers. New varieties have mainly female flowers that will produce fruit even without pollination (parthenogenesis).
Position: Bright but not in full sunlight; warm and sheltered from wind.
Propagation/planting: Sow from the beginning of the last month of spring in a temperature of at least 20ºC (68ºF). Plant two or three seeds 3 cm (1¼ in) deep in a pot with a diameter of 10 cm (4 in). Allow only the strongest seedlings to continue. If you are buying seedlings, look for low, vigorous growth, healthy leaves and a strong stem. The plants should not display any flowerbuds yet. Set young plants, no deeper than they were in their original pot, in wide containers that have a capacity of at least 10 litres (17 pints). Do not put them outside until the end of spring.

Care: Most cucumbers require support and will have to be trained. Water often and plentifully but never use water that is too cold. Cucumbers require lots of nutrients but are very sensitive to salts. Give them low doses of fertilizer.

Varieties: "Alcor", "Bella" (both pure female flowering, requiring much warmth, can tolerate mildew), "Jazzer" (mainly female flowers), "Highmark", "Sprint", "Bush Champion" (bushy growth).

Harvest: Always cut off the fruit, rather than picking. The harvest will be more abundant if you regularly harvest the fruit when it is small.

Cucumbers require a lot of water and nutrients.

A cucumber in a pot.

Courgette
Cucurbita pepo

Family: *Cucurbitaceae*.
Origin: Central America.
Botany: A fruiting vegetable that is sensitive to frost, with spreading, bushy growth. Yellow male and female flowers. Varieties with green, yellow and white fruit.
Position: Bright to fully sunny, warm and sheltered from wind.
Propagation/planting: After germination, thin out to one plant per pot. Stand young plants outside from the middle of the last month of spring.
Care: Water frequently, avoid waterlogging. Never water into opened flowers as this would stop fruit from developing. Fertilize weekly.
Plant protection: Spray on hot days to prevent powdery mildew.
Varieties: "Diamant" (green), "Gold Rush" (yellow), "Long White" (white).
Use: Raw, steamed or baked.

Honey melon
Cucumis melo

Family: *Cucurbitaceae*.
Origin: Africa, Asia.
Botany: A fruiting vegetable that requires much warmth. Climbing shoots. Yellow flowers.
Position: Full sunlight, warm and definitely sheltered from wind.
Propagation/planting: Sow from mid-spring when temperatures are at least 22°C (72°F). Plant young plants flat in containers with a capacity of 10-15 litres (17-26 pints) and do not put them outside until the end of spring.
Care: Train up a climbing frame or strings. Cut off the main shoot at a height of 1.5 m (5 ft). The fruit will appear on the secondary lateral shoots. Remove the primary lateral shoots up to a height of 50 cm (20 in); cut off higher ones above the second leaf. Allow only six fruits to remain on a plant. Water plentifully but avoid waterlogging. Give frequent low doses of fertilizer.
Varieties: "Goldstar", "Sweetheart", "Haon", "Resistant Joy" (the latter two are resistant to powdery mildew).
Harvest: Fully ripe fruit changes colour. The skin around the stalk begins to tear and the fruit becomes softer.

Courgette "Gold Rush" has yellow fruit.

An ornamental gourd.

Honeydew melon.

Green beans

Phaseolus vulgaris
(french)
Phaseolus coccineus
(runner)

Family: Leguminosae.
Origin: South and
Central America.
Botany: All beans are
sensitive to frost.
Position: Sunny to
semi-shady, sheltered
from wind.
Propagation/planting:
Sow from the middle of
the last month of spring
in temperatures of at
least 10ºC (50ºF). Grow
five to six seeds in a 10
cm (4 in) pot with a
depth of about 3-4 cm
(under 2 in). Once the
shoots are beginning to
lengthen, transplant the
plants into 5-10 litre (9-
17 pint) containers and
stand them outside from
the middle of the last
month of spring.
Care: Train runner
beans up supports.
Never allow them to dry
out (the flowers will drop
off). Avoid waterlogging.
Fertilize sparingly.
Plant protection:
Employ useful insects if
symptoms of black bean
fly or red spider mite
appear (see pp. 54-5).

Varieties
● Runner beans:
"Neckarkönigin" (green),
"Goldhilde", (yellow),
"Blauhilde" (blue),
"Selma Zebra" (striped).
● Scarlet runner beans:
"Preisgewinner" (red),
"Desirée" (white)
● Dwarf beans:
"Marona", "Bertina"
(green), "Hildora",
"Goldjuwel", "Rocdor"
(yellow), "Purpiat" (blue),
"Feuerzunge" (red
striped).
Harvest: Twice a week.
This will encourage the
formation of new
flowers.
Use: Consume only after
cooking, which breaks
down the indigestible
component phaseine.

Mange-tout
Pisum sativum

Family: Leguminosae.
Origin: Mediterranean
area, Asia Minor.
Botany: Climbing plant.
Tolerate temperatures to
-5ºC (-23ºF).
Position: Sunny, airy,
not too warm.
Propagation/planting:
Sow under cover from
the end of the first month
of spring. Plant five
seeds per 10 cm (4 in)
pot at a depth of about
4-5 cm (1½-2 in). Stand

A runner bean with blue pods.

outside in mid-spring.
Care: Train up a support
or cultivate as a hanging
plant. Water regularly;
fertilize a little.
Varieties: "Sugar Bon",
"Frühe Heinrich".
Harvest: Pick when
young.
Use: Steamed or stir-
fried. Mange-tout are
eaten with the pod.

Mange-tout flowers.

Sweet corn
Zea mays

Family: Genuine grasses (*Gramineae*).
Origin: Central America.
Botany: A tall-growing fruiting vegetable that produces one or two large cobs per plant.
Position: Sunny and warm. Too much heat will impede growth. A slight movement of air at flowering time helps pollination and the development of cobs.
Propagation/planting: Start sowing from about the end of the second month of spring. Plant two to three maize kernels at a depth of about 3-5 cm (1¼-2 in) in a pot with a diameter of 10 cm (4 in). When they have germinated, continue cultivation outside, placing the pot near a house wall to protect the plants from frost until they are ready to plant out. From the middle of the first month of summer, transplant the young plants into a container with a capacity of 10 litres (17 pints). Set them fairly deep to aid stability later on.
Care: Water regularly and fertilize weekly.

Varieties: "Aztec" (medium sweet), "Golden Supersweet" and "Early Extra Sweet" (both very sweet).
Harvest: When the fibres appears brown at the top of the cobs, they are ready to pick. At this time the entire cob, with the exception of the tip, turns yellow and a white juice is secreted if kernels are squeezed.
Use: Boil, steam or grill.

Spinach beet
Beta vulgaris

Family: Chenopodiaceae.
Origin: Mediterranean area, Asia Minor.
Botany: A biennial leaf and stalk vegetable. A distinction is made between spinach beet that is used for cutting and the larger stalked

Sweet corn.

Harvest the outer leaves of spinach beet.

spinach beet with fleshy red or white leaf stalks.
Position: Sunny to semi-shady.
Propagation/planting: Sow from the end of the second month of spring. Place two or three seeds about 3 cm (1¼ in) deep in pots with a diameter of about 5 cm (2 in), or sow by scattering and then prick out later. Stand young plants outside in 1-3 litre (2-5 pint) containers from about the middle of the last month of spring.
Care: Regularly water; fertilize weekly.

Varieties
● Stalk spinach beet: "Waliser" (white stalk) "Vulkan", "Feurio" (red stalk)
● Cutting spinach beet: "Grüner Schnitt".
Harvest: Use when freshly picked as the leaves tend to wilt rather quickly. Use only the outer leaves of stalk spinach beet and the plant will continue to produce more leaves from the inside out.
Use: Use the stalk type like asparagus, and the cutting type like spinach.

Herbs and summer flowers

Nearly all culinary herbs are easy to grow in pots and boxes and are ideal companion plants for vegetables, whether they are grown in their own pots or planted in the same box or container. As herbs do not consume many nutrients they will fit in well in mixed boxes and containers, but do best of all with vegetables that also require few nutrients.

Profusely blooming summer flowers will provide extra colour, particularly if the vegetables around them display mostly green leaf before the fruit is ripe. From the wide range of suitable herbs and summer flowers, obviously only a few can be introduced here.

Basil
Ocimum basilicum

A scented, savoury herb.
Position: Sunny, warm, no draughts.
Propagation/planting: Sow from the beginning

of the last month of spring (light-germinating seeds), and stand the pots outside two weeks later.
Care: Keep moist; fertilize sparingly.
Varieties: "Genoveser", "Dark Opal" (red leaves), "Lemon", "Red Ruffles" (curly), "Balkonstar".
Use: With tomatoes.

Borage
Borago officinalis

A savoury herb with delicate blue flowers.
Position: Sunny, but not too warm.
Propagation/planting: Sow from spring onwards. Stand outside a month later.
Care: Keep moist.
Use: Young leaves and shoot tips in salads.

Chives (left)
Allium schoenoprasum

A perennial, hardy, savoury herb.
Position: Sunny to shady.
Propagation/planting: Sow from spring onwards or divide an older rootstock when shoots appear. Place outside from mid-spring.
Care: Water plentifully; medium fertilizer.
Varieties: "Grolau".
Use: In salads or soups.

Dill
Anethum graveolens

An annual savoury herb with yellow flowers.
Position: Sunny to semi-shady.
Propagation/planting: Sow seed from the middle of spring onwards. Never transplant dill without moving the entire rootstock together with soil. Stand outside from the middle of the last month of spring onwards. Later sowing is possible.
Care: When the plants begin to flower, provide support sticks.
Varieties: "Goldkrone", "Farnblatt".
Use: Tips of leaves and flower umbels finely chopped in salads, fish dishes and sauces. Use flowers and leaves when preserving cucumbers and to enhance herb vinegars.

Lobelia

With their cushion-like growth, lobelias (*Lobelia erinus*) are particularly suitable for underplanting around vegetables.
Position: Sunny.
Propagation/planting: Sow seed from the last month of winter (light-germinating seed). Plant outside in the last month of spring.
Flowering time: From the last month of spring to the first month of autumn.
Care: Water plentifully and regularly and give low doses of fertilizer.
Varieties: "Kristallpalast", "Kaiser Wilhelm", "Saphir" (blue), "Schneeball" (white), "Rosamund" (pink).
Alternative: Alyssum (*Lobularia maritima*) is also suitable for underplanting.

Creeping zinnia

The profusely flowering creeping zinnia (*Sanvitalia procumbens*) is also very suitable for hanging containers and as an underplanting.
Position: Full sun, airy.
Propagation/planting: Sow in early spring (light-germinating seeds). Prick out three to five seedlings in 9 cm (3½ in) pots and do not keep them too warm. Plant out towards the end of spring.
Flowering time: The end of spring to mid autumn.
Care: Medium watering; low doses of fertilizer; remove dead flowers and leaves.
Varieties: "Goldteppich" (yellow), "Mandarin Orange" (orange).
Alternative: Swan River daisy (*Brachycome iberidifolia*) and *Thymophylla tenuiloba*.

Tagetes

Bushy *Tagetes* species make good companion plants for tomatoes, peppers and aubergines.
Position: Sunny, airy.
Propagation/planting: Sow seed from the first month of spring. Prick out two to three seedlings in a 9cm (3½ in) pot and plant them out at the end of spring.
Flowering time: From the end of spring to mid-autumn.
Care: Keep moist; fertilize regularly. Remove dead flowers.
Varieties: "Golden Boy", "Orange Boy", "Aurora", "Lulu".
Alternative: Upright-growing companion plants for vegetables include pinks (*Dianthus* hybrids), heliotrope (*Heliotropium arborescens*) and lady's slipper (*Calceolaria integrifolia*).

Ornamental sage

The tall flower spikes of ornamental sage (*Salvia farinacea*) are ideal for mixed boxes.
Position: Full sunlight and warm.
Propagation/planting: Sow seed indoors in the first month of spring. Prick out one or two seedlings in 9 cm (3½ in) pots and do not plant them out until the last frosts are over (during the last month of spring).
Flowering time: First month of summer to first month of autumn.
Care: Medium quantities of water and low doses of fertilizer.
Varieties: "Mina" (blue), "Argent" (white).
Alternative: Fire sage (*Salvia splendens*), coloured sage (*Salvia horminum*) and the taller growing blue sage (*Salvia patens*) are all suitable neighbours.

Position and choice

Vegetables

Name	Container	Height in cm/in	Sowing/planting Harvest	Comments
artichokes	tub	100-120 (40-48 in)	MSP/LSP LS-EA	perennial plant with blue flowers; harvest before flowering; frost-free overwintering
aubergines	box, pot/tub	50-100 (20-40 in)	MSP/LSP LS-EA	varieties with pretty violet or white flowers and fruit
beans, broad	pot/tub	150-200 (60-80 in)	MSP/LSP LS-EA	climbing; varieties with attractive red and white flowers
beans, dwarf	box, pot/tub	40-60 (16-24 in)	MSP/LSP MS-EA	varieties with green, yellow, blue and red/white striped pods
beans, runner	pot/tub	150-200 (60-80 in)	MSP/LSP MS-EA	varieties with green, yellow, blue and green/violet pods
Brussels sprouts	pot/tub	80-100 (32-40 in)	LW/LSP EA-MA	large, decorative plants; varieties with green and red sprouts and leaves
cape gooseberries	tub	100-150 (40-60 in)	ESP/LSP LS-MA	exotic plant with orange-yellow fruits; propagation from cuttings possible
courgettes	pot/tub	50-60 (20-24 in)	MSP/LSP MS-EA	varieties with yellow, green and white fruit
cucumbers	box, pot/tub	50-200 (20-80 in)	MSP/LSP MS-LS	large range of varieties; choose varieties that are not bitter
gourds	pot/tub	150-180 (60-72 in)	MSP/LSP EA-MA	many pretty shapes of fruit and colours for example, "Patison" (plate shaped)
kohlrabi	box, pot/tub	30-40 (12-16 in)	LW/MSP LSP-ES	sow in sets until beginning of LS; varieties with white and blue tubers
lettuces, cabbage/head	box, pot/tub	20-30 (8-12 in)	LW/MSP LSP	plant in sets from MSP to LS; mixed colours possible
lettuce, lamb's	box, pot/tub	5-10 (2-4 in)	LW/ESP MSP-MA	plant in sets; during summer do not stand in position that is too warm
lettuces, Romanesco	pot/tub	40-60 (16-24 in)	MSP/LSP MS	plant in sets until end ES; alternative: broccoli "Rosalind"
mange-tout	box, pot/ tub, hang. cont.	60-80 (24-32 in)	MSP/LSP ES-MS	flowers white to lilac, with delicate foliage and shoots
melons	box, pot/ tub, hang. cont.	50-200 (20-80 in)	MSP/LSP LS-MA	varieties with white, green and yellow fruit
melons, pepino	box, pot/ tub, hang. cont.	50-100 (20-40 in)	LSP LS-MA	particularly attractive hanging plants; propagate from cuttings in ESP
okra	pot/tub	70-80 (28-32 in)	MSP/ES LS	requires much warmth; use fruits cooked
peas	box, tub hang. cont.	80-100 (32-40 in)	MSP/LSP ES-MS	varieties with green and blue pods, marrow peas
peppers	box, pot/tub	40-100 (16-40 in)	ESP/LSP MS-EA	hot spicy and mild types; different fruit shapes and colours
radishes	box, pot/tub	10-20 (4-8 in)	ESP/MSP LSP-ES	continuously sow and prick out; varieties with red and red/white tubers
spinach	box, pot/tub	10-20 (4-8 in)	ESP/MSP LSP-MA	if sown in summer, risk of shooting
spinach beet	box, pot/tub	60-80 (24-32 in)	MSP/LSP MS-EA	varieties with white and red stalks; risk of shooting if temperatures too cool

Name	Container	Height in cm/in	Sowing/planting Harvest	Comments
spinach, New Zealand	box, pot/ tub, hang. cont.	20-30 (8-12 in)	MSP/LSP MS-EA	leafy veg. very sensitive to frost; harvest young shoot tips
spinach, strawberry	box, hang. cont.	20-30 (8-12 in)	ESP/MSP ES-LS	attractive, edible, red fruit; prepare leaves like spinach
sprouting vegetables, various	box, pot	5-10 (2-4 in)	MSP-MA MSP-MA	horseradish, radishes, mustard, alfalfa, cress, rucola, sunflower
sweetcorn	box, pot/tub	100-180 (40-72 in)	MSP/LSP LS-EA	attractive "ornamental" grass; whitish-red flowers
tomatoes	box, pot/ tub, hang. cont.	25-150 (10-60 in)	ESP/LSP LS-MA	plants bushy to tall; many shapes and colours of fruit

Herbs

Name	Container	Height in cm/in	Sowing/planting Harvest	Comments
basil	box, pot/ tub, hang. cont.	15-30 (6-12 in)	MSP/LSP ES-LS	varieties with green and red, smooth and curly leaves; large and small leaved types
borage	box pot/tub	40-80 (16-32 in)	MSP/LSP ES-EA	brilliant blue flowers; attracts bees
chives	box, pot/tub	30-40 (12-16 in)	ESP/MSP LSP-MA	perennial, will also thrive in shade; spherical flowerheads in second year
cress	box, pot	5-10 (2-4 in)	MSP-LSP MA	in summer on balcony; in winter on windowsill
dill	box, pot/tub	40-60 (16-24 in)	MSP/LSP ES-EA	finely feathered foliage and delicate yellow flowerheads
lemon balm	box, pot/tub	40-50 (16-20 in)	MSP/LSP ES-MA	perennial; not sensitive to cold; pleasant scent of lemons
parsley	box, pot/tub	20-30 (8-12 in)	MSP/LSP ES-EA	flowers in second year with small white umbels; curly or smooth leaves
rosemary	box, pot/tub	20-50 (8-20 in)	MW/LSP ES-MA	perennial; woody bush; keep in frostfree position; cuttings root in ESP
savory	box, pot/tub	40-80 (16-32 in)	LSP/ES ES-EA	light-germinating seeds; sensitive to frost; aromatic savoury herb with intense scent

Annual summer flowers

Name	Container	Height in cm/in	Sowing/planting Harvest	Comments
Brachycome iberidifolia Swan River daisies	box, pot/ tub, hang. cont.	15-20 (6-8 in)	ESP/LSP MS-EA	hanging; varieties with blue, violet, pink and white flowers
Dianthus hybrids pinks	box, pot/ tub	20-30 (8-12 in)	ESP/LSP ES-EA	upright growing; varieties with red, pink, violet and white flowers
Lobelia erinus lobelia	box, pot/ tub, hang. cont.	10-20 (4-8 in)	LW/LSP ES-EA	hanging; varieties with blue, pink and white flowers
Lobularia maritima rock cress	box, pot/ tub, hang. cont.	10-15 (4-6 in)	ESP/LSP ES-EA	hanging; varieties with violet, pink, and white flowers
Salvia farinacea sage	box, pot/ tub	40-50 (16-20 in)	ESP/LSP ES-EA	upright growing; varieties with blue and white flowerheads
Salvia splendens sage	box, pot/ tub	20-25 (8-10 in)	ESP/LSP LSP-EA	upright growing; strong, red flowerheads
Sanvitalia procumbens creeping zinnia	box, pot/ tub, hang. cont.	15-20 (6-8 in)	ESP/LSP ES-EA	hanging; varieties with yellow and orange flowers
Tagetes species and varieties	box, pot/ tub	20-30 (8-12 in)	ESP/LSP ES-EA	upright; varieties with yellow, orange and brown flowers

Key: ESP = early spring; MSP = mid spring; LSP = late spring; S = summer; A = autumn; W = winter

Designing with vegetables

You can really begin to experiment with planting designs when you grow vegetables on your balcony or patio. With these plants, not only the flowers but also the shapes of growth, leaf and fruit colours play an important part. The following pages will provide enchanting ideas for planting arrangements which prove that useful things can also be beautiful.

Left: This pleasant garden of flowers, vegetables and herbs is a peaceful place to sit.
Above: The lovely flowers of Coreopsis grandiflora "Early Sunrise".

Designing with vegetables

Designing with vegetables

The visual arrangement of a vegetable garden on your balcony or patio requires creativity and a liking for experimentation. Unlike classic flower plantings where you can simply copy ideas from the next balcony, the usual theories will have to be abandoned for something quite new but still both beautiful and harmonious. The pretty colours and shapes of fruit and leaves will give you lots of inspiration.

The right choice

During the balcony season, nurseries and garden centres offer a quite inexhaustible range of vegetable plants, herbs and summer flowers.
The following tips will make the choice easier for you.
● Only buy vegetables and herbs that you really like to eat.
● Some types of vegetables go really well with certain savoury herbs. If you are intending to grow tomatoes, you should also grow basil. The same goes for the partners cucumber and dill and beans and summer savory.
● Give preference to fast growing and early ripening vegetables. If you plant cabbages, you will need to be very patient while you wait to enjoy the first harvest from your

homegrown vegetable bed. Radishes and lettuce, on the other hand, can be harvested after three or four weeks, and other green sprouting vegetables require only a few days.
● The selection of vegetables suitable for balcony or patio is increasing steadily. Enquire about space-saving, compact-growing varieties.
Once you have put together a basic slection, you must also consider the aspect of visual design and add to your collection by choosing plants with attractive features. For example:
● There are particularly pretty flowers on artichokes, runner beans, courgettes and pepino melons.
● Interesting leaf shapes are supplied by lettuce, sweetcorn, dill and rosemary.
● Unusual leaf colours are offered by lettuce, spinach beet, basil and sage.
● Lovely fruit colours and shapes are found among tomatoes and gourds.
● Basil, thyme, mint and sage are particularly pleasantly scented plants.
● Exotic plants, like cape gooseberry, pepino melon, okra and strawberry spinach, are often difficult to obtain as young plants. Usually, you will have to grow them yourself from seed or cuttings.
Our tip: To your balcony vegetables add a few brilliant spots of colour in the shape of

uncomplicated summer flowers (see p. 25).

Changing arrangements

Some people who are changing over from balcony flowers to vegetables will find it hard to accept the continually altering appearance of the vegetable plants on their balconies. With vegetables, you will forever be making gaps in your display when you harvest your crop and these have to be filled again with new young plants. This means you will continue to design your arrangement throughout the whole season.

Planting on different levels

You should try to use all the available space on all levels and even plant upwards, using hanging containers and climbing frames, so that your vegetable balcony is as prolific as possible. Climbing plants that like warmth, like beans, cucumbers and gourds, will be grateful for a sheltered spot along a house wall and will reward you with a splash of colour and an abundant harvest.
Depending on their growth characteristics, arrange the plants on different levels.
● Set upright, tall-growing species, like tomatoes, peppers,

Lobelias form a colourful underplanting for vegetables and herbs.

pepino melons or sweetcorn, as dominant plants in the background.

● Medium tall, low-growing or hanging species, like lettuce, spinach beet, mange-tout, herbs and summer flowers, should be placed in the front of the container to look effective.

If you follow the basic rules of this design plan, you will make the best use of the available space without the plants interfering with each other too much. Of course, the plants themselves will never keep strictly to this plan, but this too will loosen up the total arrangement. The closer together the plants are grown, the faster the whole arrangement will blend together. However, a planting that is too densely populated risks attracting diseases.

Calculate for about one plant every 10 cm (4 in) for a balcony box. In the case of species that grow small, like lettuce, or very fast growers, like pepino melon or ornamental cabbage, the density of plants will have to be varied to suit.

Designing with vegetables

Colourful nightshade plants

The fruits of nightshade species not only provide plenty of variety with their colours, they will also offer you a varied menu.
Plants for 80 cm (32 in) boxes: 1 cape gooseberry, 1 pepper "Mavras" with violet fruit and bush-like growth, 1 pepper "Triton" with yellow fruit and bushy-compact growth, 1 sage (*Salvia officinalis*), 1 lemon thyme (*Thymus x citriodorus*), 2 *Thymophylla tenuiloba* "Goldener Fleck".
Accessories: 3-4 bamboo sticks 80-120 cm (32-48 in) long; a dianthus support ring or twine for tying up the shoots.
Planting and care: Place the cape gooseberry and both pepper plants in the background, with the herbs and summer flowers in the centre and hanging over the front. Do not stand the arrangement outside until the middle of the last month of spring. Put it in a sunny position.

A contrast of yellow and violet with nightshade and summer flowers.

Lettuces

A mixture of different lettuce types will always ensure a colourful salad bowl full of delicious surprises.

Plants for a 60 cm (24 in) box: 1 lettuce head "Sesam", 1 Batavia lettuce "Grazer Krauthäuptl", 1 oak leaf lettuce "Carnival", 1 lettuce head "Till", 1 curly lettuce "Raisa".

Planting and care: You can buy lettuce plants all through the summer or plant your own sets. Mix the different coloured lettuce varieties in two rows. Do not forget to leave a trough for watering.

Alternative: In addition to the large range of lettuces (see pp. 18-19), we also recommend mixtures with smooth and curly

Lettuces in colourful profusion.

endive or red radicchio for the autumn. Note the noticeably longer growth period of these lettuces.

A terracotta box full of lamb's lettuce

With its nutty flavour and crisp leaf rosettes, lamb's lettuce is a must for any gourmet. As it is hardy, it can also be harvested in winter.

Plants for a 40 cm (16 in) box: 8-10 seeding pots, each containing 8-10 lamb's lettuce plants. If sown out directly, distribute about 80-100 seeds evenly on the compost.

Planting and care: Sow lamb's lettuce

continuously in seed trays that contain pots with a diameter of 4 cm (1½ in). After three or four weeks, prick out the young plants into containers, spacing them about 10 × 8 cm (4 × 3¼ in) apart. Stand them in a bright but not too warm position to avoid early shooting.

Alternative: Spinach is planted in a similar way. More colour is provided by radishes which should be pricked out or sown spaced out at 6 × 6 cm (2¼ -2¼ in).

Lamb's lettuce likes to be in a container of its own.

Sweet corn and broccoli, lettuce and herbs

This attractive vegetable/herb mixture can compete with any flowerbox. Sweet corn will remain shorter in a box than when planted in the garden but will, nevertheless, look quite imposing. Together with dill, it will provide an effective arrangement.
Plants for a 60 cm (24 in) box: 4-5 sweet corn plants "Early Extra Sweet", 1 batavia lettuce "Grands Rapids Salli", 1 blue broccoli "Rosalind", 1 dill "Farnblatt", 1 red-leafed basil "Dark Opal", 1 ornamental sage (*Salvia farinacea* "Mina").
Accessories: 2-3 bamboo canes 80-120 cm (32-48 in) long if needed for the dill or sweet corn, dianthus rings for tying up.
Planting and care: The sweet corn, dill and sage should be planted in the background, the lettuce, basil and broccoli in front.
Alternative: Instead of sweet corn, you can also plant ornamental maize, for example the red "strawberry" maize

Vegetables and herbs harmoniously arranged.

or the colourful spotted variety "Harlekin". The broccoli variety "Rosalind" can also be replaced by green cauliflower "Campoverde" or by a "Romanesco" lettuce.

Curly-leafed basil in a ceramic pot

Basil comes in many different shapes of growth and colours. The variety "Green Ruffles" with curly leaves can also be obtained in purple red. Depending on the variety the range of scents runs from aniseed to lemon to cinnamon.
Plants for a 3 litre (5 pt) pot: 3 seed pots each containing 15 seedlings of basil "Green Ruffles".
Accessories: 3-4 bamboo canes 40-50 cm (16-20 in) long for tall varieties.
Planting and care: You can buy basil throughout the summer. Rarer varieties will have to be propagated from seed. Stand basil in a sunny, sheltered position.
Alternative: Pretty red-leafed herbs like Japanese mint (*Perilla frutescens*), *Atriplex hortensis* "Cupreta" and purple sage (*Salvia officinalis* "Purpurascens"), as well as the very colourful red stalk spinach beet varieties "Vulkan" and "Feurio", are very decorative.

Basil "Green Ruffles".

A rustic wooden trough with a cucumber espalier

In addition to the climbing salad cucumbers, interesting vegetable rarities provide visual pleasure in this espalier planting. Amaranth was once used by the Aztecs as a vegetable.
The oyster plant is less common with its blue-green "frosted" leaves and light blue flowers.

Plants for a 80 cm (32 in) wooden trough: 1 tall-growing salad cucumber "Bella", 1 pepper "Pusztagold", of bushy growth, 1 pepino melon "Pepino Gold", which will trail bushily, 2-3 climbing mange-tout "Frühe Heinrich", 1 oyster plant (*Mertensia maritima*), 1 violet amaranth (*Amaranthus mangostanus*), 1 lobelia (*Lobelia erinus*).

Accessories: 1 climbing frame, 180 cm × 40 cm (72 × 16 in), dianthus rings for tying up the shoots.

Planting and care: Plant the cucumber at the back in the centre and train it up the espalier. Arrange the other plants in front.

This climbing cucumber forms the background for a cheerful plant grouping.

Designing with vegetables

A colourful ensemble in a stylish wooden tub

This planting is dominated by the tall-growing dill plant with its delicate leaves and flowers. The whole effect will change in the last month of summer when the huge blue violet flowers of the artichoke compete for attention. However, if you wish to eat the artichokes you will, unfortunately, have to forego the visual delight of the flowers and eat the unopened, green buds. The flower is too tough to eat.

Plants for a tub with a diameter of 30 cm (12 in): 2 seed pots each containing 20 seedlings of dill "Fernleaf", 1 artichoke "Green Globe", 1 low-growing pepper "Festival" with yellow fruit, 1 marjoram (*Majorana hortensis*), 1 lobelia (*Lobelia erinus*).
Accessories: 1-2 bamboo canes 60-80 cm (24-32 in) long, dianthus rings for tying up, 1 inner tub made of thin plastic.
Planting and care: Those of you who wish

A delicate arrangement with dill and artichoke.

to grow your own artichokes from seed, should sow in early spring or the middle month of spring. The earlier you sow, the stronger will be its growth and the earlier the flower will appear. A temperature around 20°C (68°F) will accelerate germination. Later, the

An artichoke flower

seedlings can be pricked out into pots with a diameter of 10 cm (4 in) and can then be planted outside in their final container after the last cold days of the third month of spring. Place the dill at the back and in front of this the artichoke and the pepper. The marjoram and summer flowers should be planted in such a way that they hang over the edge. The artichoke is a hardy plant that can be overwintered in a bright, cool place at 5-10°C (2-4°F) just like rosemary. Watering during the winter should be sparing and adapted to the conditions of light. You must remove all flower stalks before bringing the artichoke indoors for the winter.
Alternative: Instead of the dill, you could also use green or bronze fennel.
Our tip: If you want the artichoke flowers to be particularly large, we recommend allowing only about five flowerbuds to remain on the plant and that you break off all the buds on the lateral shoots quite early on.

Spinach beet in a rustic willow basket

If planted as a solitary plant, spinach beet can develop into an imposing container plant. It will remain smaller if grown in a mixed planting. Bronze fennel and mange-tout will form an elegant frame for it.

Plants for a basket with a diameter of 40 cm (16 in): 1 white-stalked spinach beet "Walliser", 1 red-stalked spinach beet "Feurio", 1 fennel "Bronzefenchel", 5-6 mange-tout seedlings "Rheinische", 2 *Thymphylla tenuiloba* "Goldener Fleck", 1 blue ornamental sage (*Salvia farinacea*).

Accessories: 1-2 bamboo canes, 60-80 cm (24-32 in) long, dianthus rings for tying to.

Planting and care: Plant the spinach beet together with the other plants in the willow basket at the end of the last month of spring (see p. 11).

Alternative: Artichokes, aubergines and rosemary make imposing container plants.

Spinach beet and companion plants in a willow basket.

37

A hanging garden with cherry tomatoes

This pretty plant group in green, white and red is not merely attractive but also offers delicious ingredients for tasty meals.

Plants for a hanging container with a diameter of 25 cm (10 in): 1 balcony tomato "Tumbler", 1 basil "Rothaut", 1 white-flowering rosemary (*Rosmarinus officinalis*).

Planting and care: The best time to buy the plants is the middle of the last month of spring (at a good nursery). Distribute them evenly in the container. Make sure the hanging basket looks properly balanced.

Alternative: The selection of different hanging tomatoes is large, so try some other varieties too. Delicious tiny alpine strawberries (*Fragaria vesca*) are also ideal for planting in hanging containers.

A hanging container with cherry tomatoes and scented herbs.

Strawberry spinach in a wall basket

Strawberry spinach (*Chenopodium foliosum*, syn. *Blitum virgatum*) is an old favourite that will provide both leaves and fruit for consumption. After flowering, the shoots produce brilliant red edible fruits, looking like pearls on a string. They are reminiscent of wild strawberries but do not have a particularly characteristic flavour. In the past, this plant was grown mainly for its leaves, which were harvested when young, before flowering, and prepared in the same way as spinach. Later, the more abundant spinach took the place of this plant in many gardens.

Plants for a wall basket with a diameter of 20 cm (8 in): 2-3 seed pots each containing 5-6 seedlings.

Planting and care: Sow the strawberry spinach in sets from early spring, just like spinach. Sow the seeds directly in pots with a diameter of 10 cm (4 in) or sprinkle them over a seed tray and then prick them out

An unusual wall decoration of strawberry spinach in a willow basket.

later. After about six weeks, the seedlings can be transplanted into their final pots or containers. Stand them in a sunny to semi-shady position. The fruit will turn red around the middle of summer.

Alternative: Hanging containers planted with pepino melons are equally impressive. Even if the fruit does not ripen until the end of the summer, their attractive appearance makes up for the late harvest.

NB: Always make sure that there is a secure fixture for hanging containers as they do become very heavy.

Brilliant red fruit.

Planting and care

Vegetables grown on balconies need the best possible conditions and care if the plants are to develop well and produce a good harvest. In the following pages you will find out what is important when purchasing seeds and plants, how to grow and care for your plants and how you can keep your plants free from pests and diseases.

Left: The right tools and accessories are a useful aid for successful balcony gardening.
Above: A courgette with young fruit.

Sowing and planting

The right compost

Gardeners have been cultivating plants in pots for a long time and many special compost mixtures are on the market. Plant composts usually consist of peat, sand, loam and fertilizer. For sound ecological reasons many compost manufacturers now try to avoid using peat and, instead, mix bark and humus into plant composts. Composts can be bought containing varying amounts of fertilizer.

Seeding compost: This is a compost containing a low dosage of fertilizer, which is used for sowing seed in. Often the packaging has the words "seed compost" marked on it.

Planting compost: This is compost containing a larger proportion of fertilizer, which is used for planting young plants. It is often called "potting compost". If you have bought planting compost without any fertilizer in it, about 1 g compound fertilizer should be mixed in per litre (1¾ pints) of compost. Compost that needs a high fertilizer content requires up to 2 g per litre (1¾ pints).

Special vegetable composts Vegetables in containers require particularly good, nutrient-rich planting compost. It should also hold water, allow moisture to permeate through and remain loose and airy while still giving the plants a firm hold. You will be able to buy special composts for the cultivation of balcony vegetables in many nurseries and garden centres.

Composts containing controlled-release fertilizers: Special composts often contain controlled-release fertilizer. These fertilizers release nutrients very slowly, so that frequent additional fertilizing is not required. However, composts containing this type of fertilizer should be employed with care as the release of the nutrients is not an even process but depends, in the main, on the temperature and the moisture content of the compost.

Our tip: Choose good quality composts even if they are a little more expensive – it will pay in the end.

Making your own planting compost

Of course, you can always make up your own compost for your mini vegetable garden. The best method is to mix three parts peat, two parts each of good garden soil and ripe garden compost and one part sand. Should you wish to avoid using peat for environmental reasons, you can employ wood shreds or fibres instead. These do not, however, store water as well as peat does. To a 10 litre (17½ pint) bucket of compost add 30 g (1 oz) of an organic compound fertilizer, as well as 20-40 g (¾-1¼ oz) lime, in order to obtain the right pH value. Instead of an organic fertilizer you could also use a mineral compound fertilizer – 20 g (¾ oz) per litre (1¾ pints) compost will be quite sufficient. Make sure that everything is very well mixed.

Choosing the right seed

The quality of the seed you use is very important for the germination and healthy growth of your plants. The harvest will only be as good as the seed you bought. Take care when making your choice and read the notes on the seed packets thoroughly. All you need to know is usually written here.

Choosing the variety: When choosing your vegetables, you will need to take into account all the characteristics of the variety, like the growing time, the colour, shape, height and so on. Many varieties are particularly suitable for tubs or balcony boxes because of their compact growth. You will find notes on this in the plant descriptions on pages 14-23.

The ability to germinate: Most seeds will retain the ability to germinate for approximately two to four years but some keep only for one year. Make sure to check the "best before" date so that you know your seed is really fresh.

The seed often comes sealed in special germination-proof packets that protect it from light and moisture. This should ensure a high percentage of germination. Do not open this sort of packet until shortly before sowing the seed.

NB: Do not use vegetable seed that is too old. The germination viability date given on the packet can no longer be guaranteed once the packet has been opened.

Resistance against disease: When choosing varieties, you should also look for cultivars that are resistant to common diseases like powdery or downy mildew and other fungal infestation.

Tips when buying plants

You can grow plants from seed yourself (see pp. 44-5) or buy them as young plants from nurseries or garden centres. When purchasing young plants, you should make sure that they are healthy, strong and not too large. They should also have a good rootstock. Ask for information on the special characteristics of the variety and choose particularly disease-resistant cultivars that are suitable for growing in large containers.

Our tip: Please note that smaller seedlings grow better than larger ones.

Sprouting vegetables

It is quite easy to grow sprouting vegetables from early spring to the first frosts in autumn. They provide a regular vitamin "emergency service" with their high content of vitamins and minerals. Sprouting vegetable are seedlings with green, fully developed seedling leaves. They are grown on compost and are just a few days older than germinated sprouts. In addition to sprouted cress you can also use the seed of horse radish, radish, alfalfa, mustard and sunflowers. The small amount of space needed and the short growth time are all plus points. If sown regularly, these sprouts can be harvested continuously. Sprouting vegetables should be given a warm, sheltered spot that can be sunny to semi-shady. Flat clay dishes or balcony boxes make suitable containers. Special germination seed can often be bought from seed merchants and the specialist trade and even in wholefood and health food shops.

Method: Place compost in the seed tray and plant the seed thickly so that the seedlings will support each other in a clump when growing; 3-6 g seed is about right for a tray with a diameter of 10 cm (4 in). Cover the seed with a thin layer of compost and keep it constantly moist. After five to ten days, when green seedling leaves have developed, it is time to harvest the sprouts. Cut off the green leaves and rinse them well.

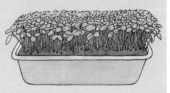

Growing and care

Sowing vegetable plants

When sowing, a distinction should be made between seed vegetables and plant vegetables. *Seed vegetables*, like radishes, many lettuces and spinach, should be sown directly into the container from which they are to be harvested later on.

Plant vegetables, like tomatoes, cucumbers, peppers, some lettuces and kohlrabi, should be planted first as seed in smaller containers or in seed trays, then pricked out or thinned out and then planted in final containers.

Growing seed and plant vegetables

Seed vegetables that are to be sown directly into a balcony box or tub should be started off as follows.
● First fill the container with compost. Carefully press the compost into the corners and brush off any excess compost.
● Mark the rows and distribute the seed at the correct spacing. This can be done carefully directly from the packet or, as with radishes, by placing individual seeds by hand.
● Finally, lightly press the seed into the compost, water carefully and cover with a thin layer of compost. A sieve is particularly useful when doing this. A watering "gully" of about 1 cm (less than ½ in) will prevent water from spilling out over the edge of the container.

Plant vegetables should be started off as follows.
● Fill a pot with a diameter of 9-11 cm (3½-4 in) or a seed tray with starter compost (see p. 42). Pat it down level and distribute the seed evenly.
● Now press the seed lightly into the compost, moisten the compost and cover the seed with a thin layer of compost.
● Mark your seeds with a label so that you will know later on what plants they are.
● Finally, stand the containers in a warm position – in spring on a windowsill, in summer in the shade of a larger container on your balcony – and keep the compost evenly moist.
● After a few days (it may take longer with some species) the seed will germinate.
● Once the seedlings are big enough for you to take hold of them with your fingers, they should be pricked out into small pots, watered and returned to their previous position.
● After three to four weeks for lettuce, six to eight weeks for tomatoes and peppers, you can transplant the young plants into their final containers.
Some large-growing species, like tomatoes and aubergines, should be potted in 10 cm (4 in) diameter pots before they are put into the final containers.

Planting out seedlings

If you have bought ready grown young seedling plants, you can plant them out right away.
Method
● Fill pots, boxes and tubs with compost. Press the compost down lightly. Leave a watering "gully" of 1-2 cm (about ½ in).
● Use a trowel to make a planting hole. Take a young plant out of its pot and place it in the hole, together with the whole rootstock. Press the plant down lightly. Biodegradable pots are planted straight into the hole.
● Then water carefully.
To ensure that the seedlings will develop properly, you should always make sure that their initial conditions are good.
Planting height: Check that you have used the right planting height. Never plant lettuces or tomatoes too deeply in the ground as this would bring a risk of decay or stalk disease.
Planting time: Many vegetable plants do not like frost and should, therefore, not be planted outside until the middle of the last month of spring. In the case of species that are particularly sensitive to the cold, like cucumber, melon and aubergine, you should have some covering material handy for cold nights. Further information on planting times can be found in the plant descriptions on pages 14-23 as well as in the planting calendar to be found on pages 26-7.

Lettuces in an amphora require little care.

Spacing: The spacing between individual plants depends on their final sizes. If you want to set radishes, herbs or flowers between the vegetable plants, you will need enough room for them to develop.
Check the following rules.
● Depending on the type of lettuce you wish to grow on your balcony, you can place up to between six and eight plants in a 80 cm (32 in) box.
● Radishes can be sown or pricked out in spaces of 6 × 6 cm (2¼ × 2¼ in).
● Four bush tomatoes will be sufficient for an 80 cm (32 in) long box. The same goes for peppers.
● Stick tomatoes, cucumbers or aubergines should, if possible, go into their own containers or boxes.

● Herbs generally do not grow very big if they are harvested regularly.

Continual sowing

Fast-growing plants, like lettuce, kohlrabi and radishes, plus spinach in spring and autumn, can be sown or planted out frequently at the right intervals of time. If you are re-using containers that have already yielded a harvest, fill them, either partly or entirely, with fresh compost.

Further care

Some fruiting vegetables, like tomatoes, cucumbers and peppers, should have their new shoots pinched out regularly once a week or at least every fortnight. These new shoots are the lateral ones emerging from the leaf axils. Pinch them out as early as possible so that all the plant's strength goes into the development of fruit. If yellow leaves form at the bottom of the plant, these should also be removed as they are often a gateway for fungal disease. Also immediately remove all damaged or deformed leaves.

Securing containers and training plants

2 Installing hanging containers: Screw fixtures securely into a wall or ceiling.

Boxes and tubs containing vegetable plants often attain a considerable weight. The secure fixing of such containers is therefore of the greatest importance, particularly in the case of hanging containers.

Securing balcony boxes
(illustrations 1a and 1b)

Always check the stability of any railing before attaching or hanging boxes on it. Use strong, safe hooks because moist compost and luxuriant plant growth will make the containers even heavier. The balance and tipping point of the box will alter considerably as the plants grow larger.
Fixtures for balcony railings: Garden centres supply fixtures for hanging boxes on the outside or inside of railings (illustration 1a). They can usually be adjusted to fit different

sizes of boxes and railings. On higher floors containers should not be attached to the outside of railings for obvious safety reasons.
Fixtures for balcony surrounds: If you intend to stand your containers on the top of a safety wall or a similar surround to a balcony, you should make absolutely sure that the fixtures are completely secure. Special corner fixtures (illustration 1b) can be obtained in the trade. These fixtures can also often be adjusted to fit different sizes of boxes and

balcony walls. Individual containers can be secured by means of battens fixed to the outside. Larger containers should always be placed on the ground. Always make absolutely sure – particularly if you are standing plant

containers in an elevated position – that all containers have a secure base.

Fixing hanging containers
(illustration 2)

Vegetable plants with trailing shoots, like pepino melon, spinach beet or hanging tomatoes, do extremely well in hanging containers. When securing them, always take into consideration the weight increase that will be caused by the fruit and screw the fixture firmly into the wall or ceiling. Fixtures on walls should also be supported from

1 Securing balcony boxes:
a Adjustable fixtures for balcony railings.
b Corner fixtures for balcony surrounds.

below, if possible. Also make sure there is enough space between the container and the wall so that the container will not bang against the wall in windy weather.

Training plants
(illustrations 3a-3c)

Vegetable plants that grow upwards require suitable climbing accessories and supports.
Sticks and strings for climbing: Plants like peppers, aubergines and, in particular, tall-growing tomatoes should be trained upwards. The best method is to tie them to bamboo canes. The main shoot should be loosely tied to its cane by means of a horizontal figure of eight loop of twine (illustration 3a). You can also train these plants upwards along simple strings (illustration 3c). For this purpose, fix hooks at the desired height in the wall or ceiling and tie the strings to them. Then wind a string loosely around the stem of the plant and tie it to

the neck of the root or to a wire loop that has been driven into the compost below. Give extra support to vegetable plants with heavier fruit by tying together two pieces of string so that two 10 cm (4 in) long ends of string

remain. As soon as the fruit becomes heavier, you can tie these string ends loosely around the stalk with the fruit.
Climbing frame: Climbers like cucumbers, peas and runner beans are best trained up supports that are simply driven into the soil or compost. In

addition, you should also fix this espalier to a wall or railing as the wall of leaves formed by the plants during the summer will create quite a resistance to wind. The shoots can be tied to the espalier with string or plant rings

made of plastic (illustration 3b).
Our tips
● Tie up your plants about once a week if possible. This is particularly important for tomatoes and cucumbers. Once chosen, the direction of training should not be changed.

● Always train runner beans anti-clockwise as they tend naturally to be left-winding.
● If possible, do this job in sunny weather to prevent the shoots from breaking too easily.

3 Tying up plants:
a Tying a stalk loosely to a stick.

b Fastening shoots to an espalier with plastic rings.

c Strings for climbing can be wound gently and loosely around the stalk.

Growing and care

An ornamental cabbage requires plenty of water.

Ripening beans should be watered sparingly.

Watering your vegetables

There should never be a very severe swing between dry and moist compost for vegetables. In our experience, small plants, in particular, are usually watered too much, while the opposite goes for tall-growing vegetable types with many leaves.

There is no hard and fast rule as to how frequently to water or how much water vegetables should have. The weather, the time of year, individual water requirements of a plant, the position and other factors should be considered. During rainy weather, plants will lose little water or none at all through evaporation. On warm days, when they are exposed to the hot sun, they will require a lot of water.

Basically, you should not pour water all over the leaves but, rather, on to the compost. Most fungal diseases are encouraged by wet foliage. In addition, the water drops act like miniature magnifying glasses in the bright sunlight and can cause burns on the leaves.

Avoid dryness and waterlogging

Wilting plants are an unmistakable sign of either watering too little or that the roots are unable to absorb water because of disease.

Tall and large plants first show signs of lack of water by allowing their heads to droop before the lower leaves begin to hang down and finally wilt.

Never water so much that water comes gushing out of the container and remains standing in the dish underneath.

All plants dislike waterlogging as it leads to decaying roots. In addition, the water running out will wash nutrients out of the compost.

Our tip: During periods of sustained rainy weather, check the plants frequently so that they are not left standing with their "feet" in water.

When to water

The best time to water by hand is in the mornings. This means that water will be available to the plants during the hours around midday when it is hottest. If you need to use the watering can again in the evening because the weather is very warm and dry, make very sure that the leaves remain dry.

How to measure the moisture in compost

In garden centres you will be able to buy measuring devices that will help you to gauge whether you are giving the right amounts of water. These moisture gauges show how well the soil is supplied with water (illustration, p. 50). These devices consist of a ceramic body, a plastic tube and a pressure gauge (manometer). In order for them to function, the ceramic cell and the plastic tube have to be filled with water and then hermetically sealed together with the manometer. The "feeler" is pushed into the container of compost that is to be checked. As the compost becomes drier, low pressure is created in the plastic tube via the porous ceramic cell and this, in turn, is registered by the manometer. The higher the needle climbs, the drier the soil. When the indicated value climbs above 50 centibars, it is definitely time to water. When the values are between 5 and 10 centibars you can delay watering. Try the gadget out on an indoor plant to get used to it and water when indicated. You will soon acquire a confident feeling for the right time to supply your plants with water.

The right water

Vegetable plants are not particularly demanding with respect to the quality of the water they receive. Mains water can be used without qualms and rainwater is just as good. Allow the water to stand for a while before watering, however, so it can warm up a little. Before connecting a rain-collecting container to your gutters and roof, do remember to have most of the dirt rinsed off the roof.

Watering equipment

An average-sized balcony will generally require a watering can holding 8-10 litres (14-17 pints). When filled, larger cans are heavier; smaller ones will need refilling constantly.

A shower attachment is useful for watering after planting.

Even a small indoor watering can is suitable. The important thing is not to give too much water too quickly so that any compost that is still fairly loose does not swell up. In the case of larger patios or roof gardens, where more extensive plantings of vegetables need to be watered, a hose will be preferable to a watering can, provided there is an outside tap.

Automatic watering

Plants in containers need to be watered more often than plants outside as their water storage capacity is limited. Today, a whole range of automatic irrigation systems exist to make your work

1 A box with a water reservoir. Wicks in the compost suck water up from the reservoir in the bottom of the box.

easier. When properly adjusted to the plants' needs, these systems will also provide the right amount of water during your absence or when you are on holiday.

Containers with a water reservoir
(illustration 1)

Balcony boxes can be bought with a water reservoir that is separated from the compost by a special inner floor. Here, the water is sucked up by the compost through wicks and replenished by means of a refill pipe. Most of these containers are also equipped with an overflow so that not too much water is given and any excess rainwater can run away. These special boxes will also enable you to cut down

watering, even on hot days, to once per day while your plants will still be well supplied with water. These containers are usually wider and higher than ordinary balcony boxes, so the fixtures must be adequate. You should also be able to obtain special interconnected balcony boxes that can be automatically supplied with water via a water tank placed above the arrangement or from a water tap. Here, too, the water is supplied to the compost via wicks. This balcony box system will require an absolutely level surface, so that an even level of water is ensured in all the containers.

Drop irrigation
(illustrations 3a-3c)

If you want to make the job of watering even easier for yourself, you can equip your plant containers with a water drop irrigation system (illustration 3a). Thin plastic hoses with drip gadgets can supply automatic watering for several containers.

Drop gadget with a clay cone (illustration 3b): In this system, the water drop device contains a hollow cone made of clay that should be filled with water. When the compost becomes dry, low pressure builds up inside the cone. This causes a valve to open enabling water to escape through the hose. These water drop devices, which are also moisture feelers, are simply pushed into the compost. Depending on requirements, they supply water or even regulate the water supply to individual plants. You can now obtain a main feeler that controls several droppers at the same time.

2 Gauges help to control the amount of moisture.

Drop devices with swollen wood feelers (illustration 3c): In this device, the tendency of wet wood to swell up is used for irrigation purposes. The drop device is equipped with a wooden part. When it becomes dry, this shrinks and activates an opening through which water can escape. As the moisture in the compost increases, the wooden part swells up again and, after a while, the opening closes once more.

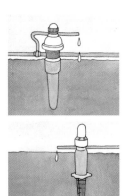

3 Automatic water drop irrigation:
a Several containers can be watered via thin plastic hoses and water drop devices. *b* A water drop device with a clay cone. *c* A water drop device with a wooden part that can swell up.

With this system, the water supply is provided either from a tank located at a higher level or from a tap. These systems work at low pressure so a pressure regulator will have to be fitted to the tap. Four or five drop devices will be required for a balcony box 1 metre (40 in) long.

Irrigation systems controlled by mains electricity

The other technically advanced irrigation systems only work with a connection to the mains water system. The water pressure has to be reduced to a maximum of 1 bar. You will also require a mains electricity point outside. This can be a proper power point, a battery or a solar cell. The amount of water is regulated through moisture sensors, called tensio switches, with respect to the duration of watering and the number of drop devices. Irrigation computers now also exist for this purpose. No limit exists on the size of the installation controlled by such expensive systems.

A water supply during your holidays

Before leaving an automatic irrigation system to its own devices, you should check how finely it needs tuning. Irrigation systems that work from a water tap should also be secured with a fail-safe device in case the hose becomes detached or bursts during your absence. The other method is to get someone to check your installation regularly so that you can avoid any unpleasant surprises on your return.

If you want to supply your plants with water from a tank for several weeks in a row you will have to ask friends or neighbours to fill the tank up again occasionally. A water tank with a capacity of 40 litres (9 gallons) will supply a 1 metre (40 in) long balcony box for about ten days.

Our tip: Enquire in a garden centre about different systems and their capabilities.

Growing and care

Correct fertilizing

During the growth period, plants constantly absorb nutrients from the compost. When cultivating plants in large containers, the limited space for the roots makes regular doses of fertilizer necessary. There follows an overview of the most important plant nutrients and fertilizers to help you to supply your vegetables with the correct nutrients.

Basic nutrients

Nitrogen (N) is the most important nutrient for a plant's growth. Adequate quantities should always be available or else the plants will become visibly light green and grow badly.
Too much nitrogen, on the other hand, will make plants soft and susceptible to pests and diseases.
Phosphorus (P) encourages plenty of flowers, ripening and root formation. Phosphorus is present in adequate quantities in most composts.
Potassium (K) strengthens the tissues and is important for a plant's stability. It makes plants less sensitive to cold and more resistant to pests and diseases.
Calcium/lime (Ca) neutralizes excess acid in composts. If too much is given it may deactivate the trace elements.

Trace elements like magnesium, boron, molybdenum and even iron are only required in minute quantities by the plants but are, nevertheless, indispensable for good development.

The most important types of fertilizer

If the above-mentioned nutrients are present singly, we speak of single nutrient fertilizers. Fertilizers containing several nutrients are far more important for balcony gardening. They are called compound fertilizers. As a rule, they contain all the important plant nutrients in a ratio to each other that may vary. Nitrogen- and potassium-rich compound fertilizers are particularly suitable for the growing of vegetables in large containers.
Fertilizers can be divided up into mineral and organic types.
Mineral fertilizers exist as single or multi-nutrient fertilizers.
● Fast-reacting mineral fertilizers contain readily soluble salts that are quickly absorbed by the plants. They come in a liquid form, as a powder or as granules. When added to water, they work faster than if they are sprinkled on to the compost in a dry form.
● Slow-reacting controlled-release fertilizers contain nutrients bound in such a way that they are released gradually through the action of water and depending on the temperature. They make constant refertilizing unnecessary.
Organic fertilizers consist mainly of animal products. The plants do not receive the nutrients until they have been broken down by soil organisms. Organic fertilization should be carried out early as it works very slowly but over a long period of time. Hoof and horn, blood and bone meal are suppliers of organic nutrients. They are sold separately or in mixtures, often together with potassium salts and phosphates. (In view of the concern over BSE (mad cow disease), it is important that you buy such products from a reputable source and wear gloves and a mask when applying them. Make sure that children do not handle them.)
● Hoof and horn fertilizers contain large amounts of nitrogen.
● Bone meal is particularly rich in phosphorus and calcium.
● Bloodmeal has a high nitrogen content and works comparatively fast.
Organic fertilizer should be strewn all round the plants and lightly worked into the compost. The compost must contain sufficient soil organisms in order for the nutrients to be released and become effective.

A luxuriant display of plants is the reward for attentive care.

Varying needs for nutrients

According to their nutrient requirements, plants can be divided into large, medium and small "feeders".

Large feeders, like tomatoes, cucumbers, gourds and sweet corn, should be fed with about 2 g compound fertilizer per plant per week during the fruit-forming period. (1 g solid fertilizer corresponds to about a level teaspoonful of liquid fertilizer.)

Medium feeders, like lettuce and spinach, require about 2-4 g of fertilizer per balcony box with a side length of 80 cm (32 in) every two weeks.

Small feeders, like radishes and many herbs, will manage on a fortnightly quantity of 1-2 g of fertilizer for a box or plant container with a length of 90 cm (36 in).

These figures should only be taken as approximate and are dependent on the compost, plants and weather conditions. They may need to be adjusted to suit individual cases.

Further tips on fertilizing

● As a rule, regular, low doses of mineral fertilizer are better than infrequent high doses. Over-fertilizing may cause burns on the roots and leaves.

● Sprinkle the fertilizer on the compost after the plants have been thoroughly watered so that the fine roots are not damaged.

● If you wish to make fertilizing an easy task, water your plants once to twice weekly with a low-dose fertilizer solution (1 g fertilizer per litre (1¾ pints) for medium feeders, 2 g for large feeders). In the case of liquid fertilizers, you should follow the dosage instructions on the packaging.

● Recently, fertilizer has also become available in the form of sticks or cones. These are pushed into the compost and release the nutrients over a longish period of time. Always use any fertilizer according to the manufacturer's instructions.

Growing and care

Natural plant protection

The most effective protection against pests or diseases is ensured by preventive measures. For this reason, choose the right position for your vegetables and adapt the supply of water and nutrients to the individual requirements of the plants. Regularly check your plants so that you will recognize infestation early on. Yellow leaves should always be removed as they are often an entry point for disease.

Preventing fungal diseases

Diseases that are caused by fungi can only be controlled by preventive measures as there are hardly any effective, non-toxic means of control. Proper watering is particularly important as moisture or wetness is, in many cases, an ideal nursery for fungal diseases. If possible, do not water plants in the evenings and avoid pouring water over the leaves. This is particularly important for lettuce, tomatoes and cucumbers.
Grey mould will affect lettuce and fruiting vegetables if they are kept too damp.
Foot and root rot is encouraged through wet leaves on tomato plants. Brown patches appear first on the leaves then on the stalks and fruit.
Downy mildew infests lettuces

and cucumbers but also melons if the leaves are often wet. Yellow- brown patches appear on the uppersides of the leaves and a whitish-grey film on the undersides.
Our tip: Ask in your local nursery or garden centre about varieties with higher resistance to downy mildew.
Powdery mildew, on the other hand, will appear if the plants are kept in very dry, warm conditions. It is recognizable by a mealy film of mould on leaves and stalks. Courgettes, cucumbers and peas, in particular, need water sprayed on them around midday on hot days to avoid this. Once a plant is infested with mildew you should remove and destroy all severely affected plant parts.

Employing useful insects

Much can be done to combat pests. The employment of useful insects is an effective and recently much more often used measure in vegetable growing. A large number of these insects can be obtained from the gardening or specialist trade.
Aphids can be controlled with a whole range of insects. In addition to lacewings, hoverflies and ladybirds that are all at home in our climatic zone, you can also employ the predatory gall midge and a wasp of the genus *Aphidius*. These useful insects

are usually delivered in the larval or pupal stage but can also be bought as mature adult insects. Always open the package in the vicinity of the infested plants so that the useful insects are released in the right place. Successful results are usually obvious after one or two weeks.
White fly occurs more often on tomatoes, peppers, aubergines and cucumbers. It is the larvae that cause the most damage. They secrete honeydew on which sooty mould spores settle to make the fruit look unappetizing. The *Encarsia* wasp can offer speedy relief. It can be purchased in the pupal stage, attached to cards that can simply be hung on the infested plants. After ten to fourteen days, success can be gauged by the fact that the white fly larvae turn black.
Red spider mites may appear on cucumbers, peppers and runner beans that are grown on house walls in warm positions. Predatory mites of the genus *Phytoseiolus* will combat these.
Thrips may also appear on vegetable plants. Help can be provided by the *Orius* wasp.
Leaf miners will sometimes appear on lettuce, tomatoes and cucumbers. The damage is caused by the larvae which eat channels through the interior of the leaves, which can lead to the death of the entire leaf if infestation is severe. Insects of the genera *Dacnusa* and

Diglyphus can be employed to control Leaf miners effectively.

Further plant protection

Plant fortification agents can be bought in garden centres to encourage the resistance of plants. They fortify the cell walls of the plants, make it more difficult for stinging and biting insects to get at the leaves and also work as a preventive against plant diseases. Beside useful insects, there are also non-toxic sprays that can be used to combat harmful insects. Only use tested agents, however, keep strictly to the manufacturer's instructions and never exceed the recommended dosage. You should always avoid employing toxic plant protection agents when growing vegetables intended for eating.

Five most common pests

Aphids
Green or black insects on leaves, stalks, shoot tips. *Occurrence:* on nearly all vegetable plants. *Useful insects:* lacewings, hoverflies, ladybirds, gall midges and *Aphidius* wasps.

White fly
Tiny white insects on leaf undersides. The larvae excrete honeydew on which colonies of sooty mould fungus appear. *Occurrence:* particularly on tomatoes, peppers, aubergines, cucumbers. *Useful insect: Encarsia* wasp.

Red spider mite
Minute, yellow-green to red creatures in fine webs. Leaves drained of sap die off. *Occurrence:* particularly on cucumbers, beans and peppers in warm positions. *Useful insects:* predatory mites (*Phytoseiolus*).

Thrips
Small, yellow to black-brown insects on leaf undersides. Their larvae suck out the leaf cells; the leaves look as if speckled with silver. *Occurrence:* on tomatoes and cucumbers. *Useful insect: Orius* wasp.

Leaf miners
2 mm (⅛ in) long yellow black insects that lay their eggs in the plant tissues. The larvae eat channels through the inside of the leaves. *Occurrence:* on lettuce, tomatoes and cucumbers. *Useful insects: Dacnusa, Diglyphus*.

Growth and care

Harvest time

In balcony and patio gardens, harvest time lasts from the second month of spring to the first frost. The first produce you will be able to harvest is cress, sprouting vegetables and chives. A little later, these are followed by radishes, lettuces and spinach. The range becomes much greater from the first month of summer onwards and hardy lamb's lettuce may bring fresh food into the kitchen even after the first frosts.

The right time to harvest

Particularly in the case of a more modest crop from a pot garden, it is important to harvest at the right time in order to obtain vegetables of the highest quality.

Fruit vegetables and legumes: You will be able to recognize the degree of ripeness by the colour of many fruit vegetables like tomatoes, peppers, aubergines and pepino melons. As a rule, they should be harvested when they are completely ripe. They will then have the best flavour and the highest vitamin content.
● Numerous fruit vegetables can be harvested several times. Always pick the young fruit of beans, peas, cucumbers and courgettes so that the season can extend as long as possible. This will encourage the formation of more fruit as the plant will not lose so much strength and therefore the harvest will be longer. Also, the smaller fruit is tastier than larger fruit from these types of vegetables.
● Some fruiting vegetables, like melons and sweet corn, have to be watched more carefully in order to recognize the right moment to harvest. More information on this can be found in the plant descriptions on pages 14-23.

Lettuce and leafy vegetables: Lettuce can be planted in sets and then harvested throughout the season. Do not allow your lettuce to get too large. This will make room for more lettuce.
● In the case of lettuce heads and spinach beet you will be able to harvest the outer leaves constantly. As long as you allow the lettuce heart to remain, new leaves will keep forming on the outside. Harvest the leaves early.
● The best tool for harvesting spinach and lettuce is a knife. Provided you do not cut too deeply, you will be able to harvest several times.

Our tip: Radishes can be harvested throughout the summer if you sow them regularly, perhaps even every week. Make sure that you pull up the radishes early enough so that they do not become woody.

The correct way to store vegetables

Occasionally you may find that your vegetable patch is overflowing and it is then time to store some of your vegetables.
● Most species of vegetables can be stored for a few days at normal temperatures in the vegetable drawer of your fridge. Delicate, sensitive lettuce and leafy vegetables will stay fresh longer in a plastic bag.
● Tomatoes, cucumbers and peppers should on no account be kept in the fridge. Temperatures of at least 12-15°C (54-59°F) are best for them.
● Spinach, peas, beans, tomatoes and other vegetables can be frozen without any problems after having been blanched briefly in boiling salted water.
● Many aromatic culinary herbs, like rosemary, lemon balm, sage, thyme, marjoram and oregano, can be dried and used to enhance dishes through the winter. Simply tie them in bunches and dry them in an airy, warm position. After that, strip the leaves and keep them cool and dry in tins or dark-coloured glass jars with screw tops.
● Other herbs, like parsley, dill and chives, will keep their flavour better if they are frozen.

The selection of tomato varieties is so great that it is difficult to make a choice. The range extends from delicate little yellow cherry tomatoes to brilliant red beef tomatoes to types with striped fruit. You can try out different varieties every year.

Index

Authors' notes

This volume deals with the care of vegetables, herbs and summer flowers on balconies and patios. This includes the handling of garden tools. Always store the latter in such a way that nobody can injure themselves. Always clear tools away immediately after use. If you sustain any injuries when working with soil or compost, please consult your physician and get expert advice on the possibility of having a tetanus vaccination. When employing fertilizers and plant protection agents, keep to the instructions on the packaging. Store these agents (even organic ones) in such a way that they are inaccessible to children and domestic animals. Consuming these substances can lead to considerable damage to health. These products should not be allowed to come into contact with your eyes. Container irrigation systems should always be installed according to the manufacturer's instructions. Elaborate systems should be installed by an expert.

Acknowledgements

The photographer and publishers wish to thank Firma Dehner, Freising, for their kind help and support.

Photographic acknowledgemnts

The photographs in this volume are by Jurgen Stork, with the exception of:
Borstell: p. 8, 24 bottom, 25 bottom, back cover; de Cuveland: p. 41 right, 48 top;
Konig: p. 3 left, 29 right;
mein schoner Garten/Krieg: p. 62;
Pforr: p. 25 top centre right;
Reinhard: p. 15 top, 16 left, right, 17 top, bottom, 18 top, 19 top, 20 left, 21 top, bottom left, 22 top, 23 top, 24 top left, 53;
Sammer: p. 3 right, 12/13, 14 top, 18 bottom, 20 right, 22 bottom, 25 top left, top centre left;
Silvestris/Brockhaus: p. 19 bottom;
Silvestris/Hanneforth: p. 14 bottom;
Stork: inside front cover, 2, 4/5, 5 right, 7, 10 top, bottom, 15 bottom, 21 bottom right, 23 bottom, 24 top centre, 25 top right, 28/29, 31, 32, 33 top, bottom, 34 top, bottom, 35, 36 top, bottom, 37, 38, 39 top, bottom, 40/41, 45, 48 bottom, 57;
Strauss: front cover;
Willner: p. 24 top right.

Cover photographs

Front cover: *A colourfully arranged balcony box with tomatoes and dahlias.*
Inside front cover: *Summery patio with vegetables and herbs.*
Back cover: *Lettuce and peppers ripe for harvesting in decorative containers.*

This edition published 1997 by Merehurst Limited
Ferry House, 51-57 Lacy Road, Putney, London SW15 1PR

© 1995 Gräfe und Unzer GmbH, Munich

ISBN 1 85391 632 3

English text copyright © Merehurst Limited 1997
Translated by Astrid Mick
Edited by Lesley Young
Design and typesetting by Paul Cooper Design
Printed in Hong Kong by Wing King Tong

Decorative plants

A colourful multitude of shapes and forms can be found in these two members of the cabbage family, cauliflower and broccoli. This pair are generally a little more demanding with respect to care. Regular watering is particularly important. As large feeders they also require sufficient nutrients and a loose compost. Attentive care will be rewarded with a tasty, vitamin-rich harvest. Grown in pots, the attractive flowering heads generally remain smaller than those of plants grown in gardens. The "flowers" of broccoli can be harvested over a longer period of time. If you cut out the main shoot in time, lateral shoots with new heads will form.
As growing your own plants from seed is not always easy, it is a good idea to purchase young plants from a good nursery.

A colourful arrangement of white and green cauliflower with purple and green broccoli.

Other titles available in the series

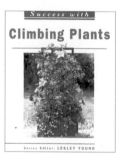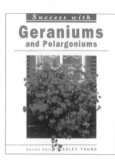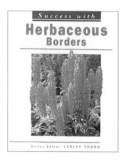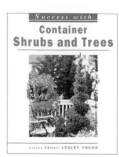